Contents

W9-DEG-526

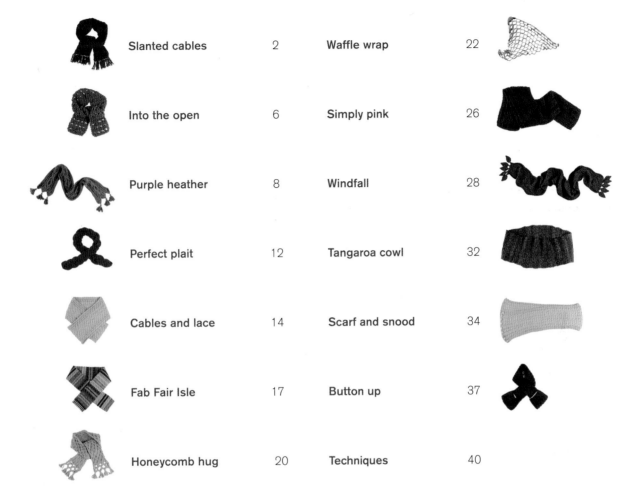
Introduction

The versatile scarf is the perfect accessory to complete any outfit, and any of these inspirational designs will brighten the day, no matter how grey. So grab those needles and knit one or more for yourself or as a unique gift for a treasured friend.

These scarves are fun and easy to make, and every project is accompanied by clear instructions describing how to achieve perfect results. You can follow them to the letter or use them as a basis for your own creations. In addition, a techniques section explains all the basic skills needed, making them suitable for experienced knitters and novices alike. Quick to knit, these designs are an ideal way of using up oddments of yarn and make perfect portable projects for knitters on the go. We're sure you'll enjoy making them.

Slanted cables

Work a new slant on classic cables with this wool creation. You'll increase on both sides of the scarf to the maximum stitch count, then decrease down the other side. Finish with double crochet and a fringe.

SIZE
- Approx 8 x 79in (20 x 200cm) (not including fringe)

MATERIALS
- Classic Collection 100% Pure Wool DK (137yd/125m per 50g ball): 7 balls in 1009
- A pair of 4mm (UK8:US6) needles
- A 3.5mm (UK9:USE/4) crochet hook

TENSION
Not critical. Yarn band tension: 22 sts and 28 rows to 4in (10cm) over st st using 4mm needles.

SPECIAL ABBREVIATIONS
C6B (cable 6 back): Slip 3 sts on to cable needle and hold to back of wk, k3, then k3 from cable needle.

SCARF
Cast on 1 st, knit and mark this st.

Row 1: Inc in this st (2 sts).

Row 2: Inc in each of these 2 sts (4 sts).

Row 3: Inc in first st, k to last st, inc in last st (6 sts).

Row 4: As row 3 (8 sts).

Row 5 (WS): Inc in first st, p6, inc in last st (10 sts).

Row 6: Inc in first st, k1, C6B, k1, inc in last st (12 sts).

Row 7: Inc in first st, k2, p6, k2, inc in last st (14 sts).

Row 8: Inc in first st, k to last st, inc in last st (16 sts).

Row 9: Inc in first st, k4, p6, k4, inc in last st (18 sts).

Row 10: As row 8 (20 sts).

Row 11: Inc in first st, k6, p6, k6, inc in last st (22 sts).

Row 12: Inc in first st, k7, C6B, k7, inc in last st (24 sts).

Row 13: Inc in first st, p2, k6, p6, k6, p2, inc in last st (26 sts).

Row 14: As row 8 (28 sts).

Row 15: Inc in first st, p4, k6, p6, k6, p4, inc in last st (30 sts).

Row 16: As row 8 (32 sts).

Row 17: Inc in first st, (p6, k6) twice, p6, inc in last st (34 sts).

Row 18: Inc in first st, k1, (C6B, k6) twice, C6B, k1, inc in last st (36 sts).

Row 19: Inc in first st, k2, (p6, k6) twice, p6, k2, inc in last st (38 sts).

Row 20: As row 8 (40 sts).

Row 21: Inc in first st, k4, (p6, k6) twice, p6, k4, inc in last st (42 sts).

Row 22: As row 8 (44 sts).

Row 23: Inc in first st, (k6, p6) 3 times, k6, inc in last st (46sts).

Row 24: Inc in first st, k1, (k6, C6B) 3 times, k7, inc in last st (48 sts).

Row 25: Inc in first st, p2, (k6, p6) 3 times, k6, p2, inc in last st (50 sts).

Row 26: As row 8 (52 sts).

Row 27: Inc in first st, p4, (k6, p6) 3 times, k6, p4, inc in last st (54 sts).

Row 28: As row 8 (56 sts).

Row 29: Inc in first st, (p6, k6) 4 times, p6, inc in last st (58 sts).

Row 30: Inc in first st, k1, (C6B, k6) 4 times, C6B, k1, inc in last st (60 sts).

Row 31: Inc in first st, k2, (p6, k6) 4 times, p6, k2, inc in last st (62 sts).

Row 32: As row 8 (64 sts).

Row 33: Inc in first st, k4, (p6, k6) 4 times, p6, k4, inc in last st (66 sts).

Row 34: As row 8 (68 sts).

Row 35: Inc in first st, (k6, p6) 5 times, k6, inc in last st (70 sts).

Row 36: Inc in first st, k1, (k6, C6B) 5 times, k7, inc in last st (72 sts).

Row 37: Inc in first st, p2, (k6, p6) 5 times, k6, p2, inc in last st (74 sts).

Row 38: As row 8 (76 sts).

Row 39: Inc in first st, p4, (k6, p6) 5 times, k6, p4, inc in last st (78 sts).

Row 40: As row 8 (80 sts).

Row 41: Inc in first st, (p6, k6) 6 times, p6, inc in last st (82 sts).

Row 42: Inc in first st, k1, (C6B, k6) 6 times, C6B, k1, inc in last st (84 sts).

Row 43: Inc in first st, k2, (p6, k6) 6 times, p6, k2, inc in last st (86 sts).

Row 44: As row 8 (88 sts).

Row 45: Sl1, k1, psso, k3, (p6, k6) 6 times, p6, k4, inc in last st.

Row 46: Inc in first st, k to last 2 sts, k2tog.

Row 47: Sl1, k1, psso, k1, (p6, k6) 7 times, inc in last st.

Row 48: Inc in first st, k1, (k6, C6B) 7 times, k2 tog.

Row 49: Sl1, k1, psso, p5, (k6, p6) 6 times, k6, p2, inc in last st.

Row 50: As row 46.

Row 51: Sl1, k1, psso, p3, (k6, p6) 6 times, k6, p4, inc in last st.

Row 52: As row 46.

Row 53: Sl1, k1, psso, p1, (k6, p6) 7 times, inc in last st.

Row 54: Inc in first st, k1, (C6B, k6) 7 times, k2tog.

Row 55: Sl1, k1, psso, k5, (p6, k6) 6 times, p6, k2, inc in last st.

Row 56: As row 46 (88 sts).

Rep rows 45 to 56 until scarf measures approx 79in (200cm), ending with row 52.

Next row: Sl1, k1, psso, p1, (k6, p6) 7 times, k1 (87 sts).

Next row: K1, (C6B, k6) 7 times, k2tog (86 sts).

Next row: Sl1, k1, psso, k5, (p6, k6) 6 times, p5, k2tog (84 sts).

Next row: Sl1, k1, psso, k to last 2 sts, k2tog (82 sts).

Next row: Sl1, k1, psso, k3, (p6, k6) 6 times, p3, k2tog (80 sts).

Keeping the patt as set, continue to decrease at each end of every row until 2 sts rem.

K2tog and fasten off.

FINISHING

Starting with the one remaining st and using a 3.5mm hook, wk a row of double crochet all around the edge of the scarf. Use the remaining wool to make a tasselled fringe at each end (see page 47 for details).

Into the open

The fancy openwork stitch used on this scarf is a lot easier to knit than it looks. The strands are elongated and crossed to produce a fabric that is both open and warm.

SIZE
- Approx 8 x 100in (20 x 254cm)

MATERIALS
- Cygnet Seriously Chunky 100% Acrylic (52yd/48m per 100g ball): 4 balls in 4888 Burnt Orange
- A pair of 10mm (UK000:US15) needles

TENSION
Not critical. Ball band tension: 6 sts and 9 rows to 4in (10cm) over st st using 10mm needles.

SCARF
Cast on 14 sts.
Commence patt
Row 1: Knit.
Row 2: Knit.
Row 3: K1, knit to last stitch wrapping the yarn around the needle 4 times for each stitch, k1.
Row 4: K1, *pass next 3 sts to right-hand needle, dropping extra loops, pass these 3 sts back on to left-hand needle, and (k3tog without slipping sts from needle, p3tog into same sts without slipping sts from needle, k3tog into same sts and slip sts from needle), rep from * to last st, k1.
These 4 rows form patt.
Cont in patt until wk measures 100in (254cm) from beg, ending with row 4.
Knit 2 rows.
Cast off.

Purple heather

Texture abounds in this chunky neck wrapper, packed with twist stitches, cables and bobbles. The finishing touch is added with garter stitch triangles and jaunty tassels.

SIZE
- Approx 10¼ x 64½in (26 x 164cm), excluding tassels

MATERIALS
- Hayfield Bonus Aran 80% acrylic, 20% wool (919yd/840m per 400g ball): 1 ball in 871 Purple Heather
- A pair each of 8mm (UK0:US11) and 7mm (UK2:US10.5) needles
- Cable needle

TENSION
Not critical. Yarn band tension: 12 sts and 16 rows to 4in (10cm) over st st with yarn used double, using 8mm needles.

SPECIAL ABBREVIATIONS
- MB (make bobble): (P1, k1, p1, k1, p1) all into next st, pass the 2nd, 3rd, 4th and 5th sts (one at a time) over the first st
- C8B (cable 8 back): Slip next 4 sts on to cable needle and leave at back of work, k4, then k4 from cable needle
- C8F (cable 8 front): Slip next 4 sts on to cable needle and leave at front of work, k4, then k4 from cable needle
- TW2R (twist 2 right): Knit into 2nd st on left needle, then knit the first st, sl both sts off left needle together

PATTERN NOTES
Wind yarn into two equal-sized balls before knitting. Yarn is used double throughout main part of scarf, and single for triangular edging.

SCARF
Using larger needles and doubled yarn, cast on 40 sts.

Row 1 (RS): *K2, p2, rep from * to end.

Wk 3 rows more in rib.

Commence patt

Row 1 (RS): K2, p4, TW2R, p2, MB, p1, k16, p1, MB, p2, TW2R, p4, k2.

Row 2: P2, k4, p2, k4, p16, k4, p2, k4, p2.

Row 3: K2, p4, TW2R, p2, MB, p1, C8B, C8F, p1, MB, p2, TW2R, p4, k2.

Row 4: As row 2.

Rows 5 to 10: Rep rows 1 and 2 three times.

Rows 11 and 12: As rows 3 and 4.

Rows 13 to 18: Rep rows 1 and 2 three times.

Row 19: K2, p4, TW2R, p2, MB, p1, C8F, C8B, p1, MB, p2, TW2R, p4, k2.

Row 20: As row 2.

Rows 21 to 26: Rep rows 1 and 2 three times.

Rows 27 and 28: As rows 19 and 20.

Rows 29 to 32: Rep rows 1 and 2 twice. These 32 rows form patt.

Cont in patt until scarf measures 63in (161cm) from beg, ending with row 32. Wk 4 rows in k2, p2 rib as before. Cast off.

Divide cast-on and cast-off edges into three and place markers to indicate position of triangles.

TRIANGULAR EDGING
First triangle
Using smaller needles, one strand of yarn, and with RS facing, pick up and k13 sts across cast-on edge to first marker for first triangle.
Knit 3 rows.
Row 1 (RS): K1, k2tog, k to last 3 sts, sl1, k1, psso, k1.
Row 2: Knit.
Rep rows 1 and 2 until 5 sts rem, ending with WS row.
Next row: K1, k3tog, k1.
Next row: K3tog and fasten off.

Middle triangle
Using smaller needles, one strand of yarn, and with RS facing, pick up and k13 sts between markers, skipping 1 st at centre.
Wk as given for first triangle.

Third triangle
Using smaller needles, one strand of yarn, and with RS facing, pick up and k13 sts from second marker to end.
Wk as given for first triangle.
Wk triangular edging across cast-off edge in the same manner.

FINISHING
Make six tassels (see page 46 for details) and attach to ends of triangles.

Perfect plait

This garter-stitched and plaited scarf combines dramatic effect with simplicity. Two methods are given, the second being slightly more complex than the first. Why not try them both?

SIZE
- Approx 3 x 52in (8 x 132cm)

MATERIALS
- Adriafil Carezza 70% Angora, 20% Polyamide, 10% Wool (91yd/83m per 25g ball): 3 balls in 22 Blu
- A pair of 4.5mm (UK7:US7) needles (2 pairs for Method 2)
- Stitch holders (for Method 2 only)

TENSION
Not critical. Ball band tension: 17 sts and 24 rows to 4in (10cm) on 5.5mm needles.

PATTERN NOTES
Any weight or colour of yarn can be used. When you have three strips of equal length, plait them together. Plaiting will reduce the overall length by one-third, so if each strip is 60in (153cm) in length, your finished scarf will be 40in (102cm) when plaited.

METHOD 1
Cast on 10 sts.
Knit every row until wk measures 78in (200cm) or desired length.
Cast off.
Rep twice more.
Place the three strips on top of each other and sew the three cast-on ends together.
Plait evenly (it's easiest on a flat surface, such as the floor or a table) and sew together the three cast-off ends.

METHOD 2
Cast on 10 sts.
Knit every row until wk measures 78in (200cm) or desired length is achieved.
Place sts on a holder.
Pick up and knit 10 sts from the cast-on edge of the first strip and knit every row until wk measures same as first strip.
Place sts on st holder.
Pick up and knit 10 sts from the same cast-on edge as before and complete as before.
Place sts on st holder.
Plait the three strips evenly.
Return the sts to three separate needles and lay them on top of each other.
Using a fourth needle, cast off the sts of the three strips together.

Cables and lace

This cable combination worked up in a lovely pale neutral colour makes a classic scarf for any season. Slipping the first stitch of every row creates a nice crisp edge.

SIZE
- Approx 12½ x 64in (32 x 162.5cm)

MATERIALS
- Artesano Aran 50% Alpaca, 50% Peruvian Highland Wool (144yd/132m per 100g skein): 4 skeins in CA03 Maple
- A pair of 5mm (UK6:US8) needles
- Cable needle
- Tapestry needle

TENSION
Not critical. Yarn band tension: 17 sts and 21 rows to 4in (10cm) over st st using 5mm needles.

SPECIAL ABBREVIATIONS
- C4B (cable 4 back): Slip next 2 sts on to cable needle and hold to back of wk, k2 then k2 from cable needle
- T4B (twist 4 back): Slip next 2 sts on to cable needle and hold to back of wk, k2 then p2 from cable needle
- T4F (twist 4 front): Slip next 2 sts on to cable needle and hold to front of wk, p2 then k2 from cable needle

PATTERN NOTES
Instructions are given in written and chart form, but produce the same design. Choose whichever method of working you prefer.

SCARF
Cast on 48 sts using the thumb method.

Commence patt from written instructions
Row 1 (RS): Sl1, k1, p3, k2tog, k1, yo, k1, yo, k1, ssk, p6, k4, p4, k4, p6, k2tog, k1, yo, k1, yo, k1, ssk, p3, k2.
Row 2: Sl1, k4, p7, k6, p4, k4, p4, k6, p7, k5.
Row 3: Sl1, k1, p3, k2tog, yo, k3, yo, ssk, p6, C4B, p4, C4B, p6, k2tog, yo, k3, yo, ssk, p3, k2.
Row 4: As row 2.
Row 5: Sl1, k1, p3, k1, yo, ssk, k1, k2tog, yo, k1, p6, k4, p4, k4, p6, k1, yo, ssk, k1, k2tog, yo, k1, p3, k2.
Row 6: As row 2.
Row 7: Sl1, k1, p3, k2, yo, sl1, k2tog, psso, yo, k2, p6, C4B, p4, C4B, p6, k2, yo, sl1, k2tog, psso, yo, k2, p3, k2.
Row 8: As row 2.
Row 9: Sl1, k1, p3, k2tog, k1, yo, k1, yo, k1, ssk, p4, T4B, T4F, T4B, T4F, p4, k2tog, k1, yo, k1, yo, k1, ssk, p3, k2.
Row 10: Sl1, k4, p7, k4, p2, k4, p4, k4, p2, k4, p7, k5.
Row 11: Sl1, k1, p3, k2tog, yo, k3, yo, ssk, p4, k2, p4, C4B, p4, k2, p4, k2tog, yo, k3, yo, ssk, p3, k2.
Row 12: As row 10.

CABLES AND LACE CHART

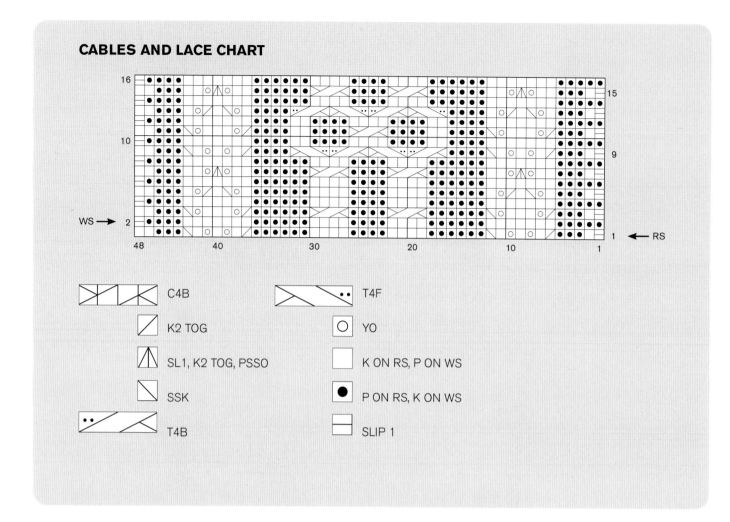

	C4B		T4F
	K2 TOG	O	YO
	SL1, K2 TOG, PSSO		K ON RS, P ON WS
	SSK	●	P ON RS, K ON WS
	T4B		SLIP 1

Row 13: Sl1, k1, p3, k1, yo, ssk, k1, k2tog, yo, k1, p4, T4F, T4B, T4F, T4B, p4, k1, yo, ssk, k1, k2tog, yo, k1, p3, k2.

Row 14: Sl1, k4, p7, k6, p4, k4, p4, k6, p7, k5.

Row 15: Sl1, k1, P3, k2, yo, sl1, k2tog, psso, yo, k2, p6, C4B, p4, C4B, p6, k2, yo, sl1, k2tog, psso, yo, k2, p3, k2.

Row 16: As row 14.

These 16 rows form patt.

Commence patt from chart

Starting with row 1, wk 16 rows as given on chart.

Both written instructions and chart

Cont in patt until work measures approx 64in (162.5cm) from beg, ending with row 16. Cast off using the sewn cast-off method. To do this, cut a tail three times the width of the knitting and thread it on to a tapestry needle. *Pass through the first two stitches p-wise. Pass through the first stitch from left to right. Pull the yarn through and drop the first stitch from the needle. Repeat from * until all stitches are cast off.

FINISHING

Block the scarf to measurements given as follows: pin out and lightly spray with water all over. Leave in place until completely dry.

Fab Fair Isle

Based on traditional Fair Isle motifs, this design was inspired by a scarf in the Shetland Museum in Scotland. Its vibrant pattern remodels these long-established ideas on a larger scale and in bold colours.

SIZE
- Approx 6½ x 62in (16.5 x 158cm)

MATERIALS
- Cascade 220 DK 100% Peruvian Highland wool (220yd/200m per 100g skein); 1 skein in each of the following shades:
- 9076 Mint (A)
- 9427 Duck Egg Blue (B)
- 7812 Lagoon (C)
- 7813 Jade (D)
- 5018 Summerdaze (E)
- 9455 Turquoise Heather (F)
- 2433 Pacific (G)
- 4009 Teal (H)
- A 4.5mm (UK7:US7) 16in (40.5cm) circular needle

TENSION
- 20 sts and 28 rows to 4in (10cm) over st st using 4.5mm needles.
- Use larger or smaller needles to obtain correct tension.

PATTERN NOTE
Strand yarn loosely across back of work, keeping the fabric elastic.

SCARF
Using E cast on 80 sts.
Join for working in the round.
Round 1: *K2 E, p2 D, rep from * to end.
Work 9 rounds more in corrugated rib as set in round 1.

Commence chart
Working in st st, starting with round 1, and repeating the 20 sts 4 times, wk rounds 1 to 136 of charts 3 times, then wk the final 6 rounds once.

Commence rib
Wk 10 rounds of corrugated rib as follows:
Round 1: *K2 A, p2 H, rep from * to end.
Wk 9 rounds more in corrugated rib as set.
Using A cast off loosely in rib.

FAIR ISLE ROUNDS 1–70

FAIR ISLE ROUNDS 71–136 (+6)

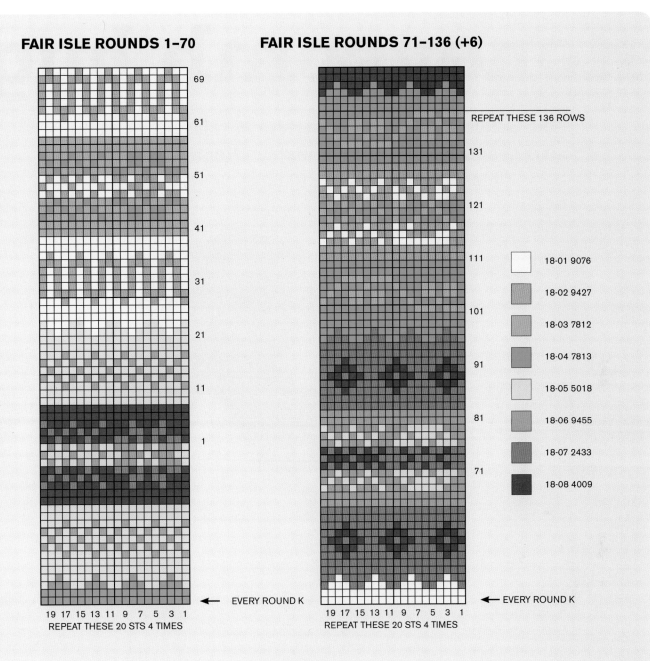

REPEAT THESE 136 ROWS

← EVERY ROUND K

← EVERY ROUND K

19 17 15 13 11 9 7 5 3 1
REPEAT THESE 20 STS 4 TIMES

19 17 15 13 11 9 7 5 3 1
REPEAT THESE 20 STS 4 TIMES

18-01 9076
18-02 9427
18-03 7812
18-04 7813
18-05 5018
18-06 9455
18-07 2433
18-08 4009

Honeycomb hug

The textured honeycomb pattern in this extra chunky scarf is easy to master and highly effective. The design is finished off with a distinctive knotted fringe.

SIZE
- Approx 6 x 68in (15 x 173cm), excluding fringe

MATERIALS
- Cygnet Seriously Chunky 100% Acrylic (52yd/48m per 100g ball): 5 balls in 4884 Barley
- A pair of 9mm (UK00:US13) needles
- Cable needle
- A large crochet hook

TENSION
13 sts and 12 rows to 4in (10cm) over patt using 9mm needles. Use larger or smaller needles to obtain correct tension.

SPECIAL ABBREVIATIONS
- T3F (twist 3 front): Slip next stitch on to cable needle and hold to front of work, p2, then k1 from cable needle
- T3B (twist 3 back): Slip next 2 stitches on to cable needle and hold to back of work, k1, then p2 from cable needle

SCARF
Cast on 20 sts.

Commence patt
Row 1 (RS): K2, *p4, k2, rep from * to end.
Row 2: P2, *k4, p2, rep from * to end.
Row 3: K1, *T3F, T3B, rep from * to last st, k1.
Row 4: K3, p2, *k4, p2, rep from * to last 3 sts, k3.
Row 5: P3, k2, *p4, k2, rep from * to last 3 sts, p3.
Row 6: As row 4.
Row 7: K1, * T3B, T3F, rep from * to last st, k1.
Row 8: As row 2.
These 8 rows form patt.
Cont in patt until scarf measures approx 68in (172cm) in length, ending with row 1.
Cast off.

FRINGE
Cut 32 lengths of yarn to twice the desired length of fringe plus 1in (2.5cm). Divide into groups of four strands.
Using a crochet hook to pull yarn through a stitch at cast-on edge, draw centre of strands through, forming a loop. Draw ends through loop to create first tassel. Add three more tassels across cast-on edge. Knot tassels to form fringe as shown in photograph.
Create fringe across cast-off edge in the same way.

Waffle wrap

Don't let the complicated appearance of this grid deter you from trying it out. Once you have needles and yarn in hand, this scarf of interlocking tiers is easy and fun to knit.

SIZE
The scarf forms a triangle, approx 67in (170cm) on longest side and 39in (100cm) from longest side to apex point.

MATERIALS
- Patons 100% cotton DK (230yd/210m per 100g ball): 4 balls in 2714 Raffia (MC); 4 balls in 2692 Cream (CC)
- A pair of 4mm (UK8:US6) needles
- A 4mm double-pointed 4mm (UK8:US6) needle

TENSION
Not critical. Yarn band tension: 22 sts and 30 rows to 4in (10cm) over g-st using 4mm needles.

PATTERN NOTES
The texture of this pattern is produced by a series of strips or tiers, which each have a sequence of knit and purl rows, creating a waffle effect. The strips gradually broaden and the spaces between them gradually get longer. Strips are knitted together rather than sewn, which gives a more even finish and allows the scarf to drape flexibly. It can be worn in a number of ways.

Throughout pattern, slip first st of every row, k into back of last st of every row.

The number of sts in the rows is given at the beginning of the instructions for each tier.

SPECIAL INSTRUCTIONS
Pick-up row 1
Before you start this row, fold the knitting so that the strip you are currently knitting is on top of the strip in the alternate colour. Look for the first three rows of rev st st. The middle row should be marked and is the one to pick up. Using a double-pointed needle, pick up the top of each st, except the first and last. Hold this needle behind the left-hand needle. K1, *k tog 1 st from each needle, rep from * to last st, k1 tbl.

Pick-up and cast-off
Wk as for pick-up row. Sl first st of the row you are working, then sl 1 from cable needle on to left-hand needle, k tog with next st. Repeat, casting off as you go.

Pick-up row 2
This row will be worked into the first marked row of the tier just completed, the middle row of the first 3-row rev st st section. Pick up into the top of the sts in

this row as directed – this may be the same number or 1 or 2 fewer sts than the original row and will be indicated in the pattern. Begin working row 1 from the double-pointed needle.

Pick-up row with increase

Wk as for pick-up row 2, but when picking up sts to start, pick up all but the first st on the marked row. Then inc 1 by knitting into front and back of first st, k the row as given for the pick-up row, inc into last st. You have now increased the number of sts in the row by 1.

SCARF

Tier 1

Using MC cast on 10 sts.

Rows 1: Purl.
Row 2: Purl.
Row 3: Knit.
Rows 4 to 7: Rep rows 2 and 3 twice.
Row 8: Knit.
Row 9: Purl.
Rows 10 to 13: Rep rows 8 and 9 twice.
Row 14: Purl.
Row 15: Knit.
Row 16: Purl.
Rows 17 to 28: As rows 2 to 13.
Row 29: Purl.
Row 30: Knit (this row will be picked up by the next tier, so mark with a st marker or yarn scrap of another colour).
Rep these 30 rows 14 times more.
On the final rep, you do not need to mark the last row.

Tier 2

Change to CC.

Row 1: Purl.
Row 2: Purl.
Row 3: Knit.
Rows 4 to 7: Rep rows 2 and 3 twice.
Row 8: Knit.
Row 9: Purl.
Rows 10 to 13: Rep rows 8 and 9 twice.
Row 14: Purl.
Row 15: Knit and mark this row.
Row 16: Purl.
Rows 17 to 28: As rows 1 to 12.
Row 29: Purl.
Row 30: Wk Pick-up row 1 (see special

instructions). Note: You'll be picking up the marked row of the last section of Tier 1. As you work through Tier 2, wk pick-up rows into each subsequent marked row of Tier 1. Rep these 30 rows 13 times more, then wk rows 1 to 29 once.
Fold your work so that Tier 2 is on top of Tier 1 and the original cast-on row from Tier 1 is under the needle. The two sections should be the same length.
Wk Pick-up and cast-off row, picking up into the cast-on (see special instructions).

Tier 3

Using MC wk Pick-up row 2 (10 sts).
Wk rows 1 to 30 as given for Tier 2 fourteen times.
On the final rep, wk Pick-up and cast-off row instead of Pick-up row 1.

Tier 4

Using CC wk Pick-up row 2 (10 sts).
Wk rows 1 to 30 as given for Tier 2 thirteen times.
On the final rep, wk Pick-up and cast-off row instead of Pickup row 1.

Tier 5

Using MC wk Pick-up row with increase (see special instructions) (11 sts).
Wk rows 1 to 30 as given for Tier 2 twelve times.
On the final rep, wk Pick-up and cast-off row instead of Pick-up row 1.

Tier 6

Using CC wk Pick-up row 2 (11 sts).
Row 1: Purl.
Row 2: Purl.
Row 3: Knit.
Rows 4 to 7: Rep rows 2 and 3 twice.
Row 8: Purl.
Row 9: Purl.
Row 10: Knit.
Rows 11 to 14: Rep rows 9 and 10 twice.
Row 15: Purl.
Row 16: Purl.
Row 17: Knit and mark this row.
Row 18: Purl.
Rows 19 to 32: As rows 2 to 15.
Row 33: Purl 1 row
Row 34: Wk Pick-up row 1.
Rep these 34 rows 10 times more.
On the final rep, wk Pick-up and cast-off row instead of Pick-up row 1.

Tier 7

Using MC, wk Pick-up row 2 (11 sts).
Wk rows 1 to 34 as given for Tier 6 ten times.
On the final rep, wk Pick-up and cast-off row instead of Pick-up row 1.

Tier 8

Using CC, wk Pick-up row with increase (12 sts).
Wk rows 1 to 34 as given for Tier 6 nine times.
On the final rep, wk Pick-up and cast-off row instead of Pick-up row 1.

Tier 9

Using MC, wk Pick-up row 2 (12 sts).
Row 1: Purl.
Row 2: Purl.
Row 3: Knit.
Rows 4 to 9: Rep rows 2 and 3 three times.
Row 10: Knit.
Row 11: Purl.
Rows 12 to 17: Rep rows 10 and 11 three times.
Row 18: Purl.
Row 19: Knit and mark this row.
Row 20: Purl.
Rows 21 to 36: As rows 2 to 17.
Row 37: Purl.
Row 38: Wk Pick-up row 1.
Rep these 38 rows 7 times more.
On the final rep, wk Pick-up and cast-off row instead of Pick-up row 1.

Tier 10

Using CC, wk Pick-up row with increase (13 sts).
Wk rows 1 to 38 as given for Tier 9 seven times.
On the final rep, wk Pick-up and cast-off row instead of Pick-up row 1.

Tier 11

Using MC, wk Pick-up row 2 (13 sts).
Wk rows 1 to 38 as given for Tier 9 six times.
On the final rep, wk Pick-up and cast-off row instead of Pick-up row 1.

Tier 12

Using CC, wk Pick-up row with increase (14 sts).
Row 1: Purl.
Row 2: Purl.

Row 3: Knit.

Rows 4 to 9: Rep rows 2 and 3 three times.

Row 10: Purl.

Row 11: Purl.

Row 12: Knit.

Rows 13 to 18: Rep rows 11 and 12 three times.

Row 19: Purl.

Row 20: Purl.

Row 21: Knit and mark this row.

Row 22: Purl.

Rows 23 to 40: As rows 2 to 19.

Row 41: Purl.

Row 42: Wk Pick-up row 1.

Rep these 42 rows four times more.

On the final rep, wk Pick-up and cast-off row instead of Pick-up row 1.

Tier 13

Using MC, wk Pick-up row 2 (14 sts).

Wk rows 1 to 42 as given for Tier 12 four times.

On the final rep, wk Pick-up and cast-off row instead of Pick-up row 1.

Tier 14

Using CC wk Pick-up row with increase (15 sts).

Wk rows 1 to 42 as given for Tier 12 three times.

On the final rep, wk Pick-up and cast-off row instead of Pick-up row 1.

Tier 15

Using MC, wk Pick-up row 2 (15 sts).

Row 1: Purl.

Row 2: Purl.

Row 3: Knit.

Rows 4 to 11: Rep rows 2 and 3 four times.

Row 12: Knit.

Row 13: Purl.

Rows 14 to 21: Rep rows 12 and 13 four times.

Row 22: Purl.

Row 23: Knit and mark this row.

Row 24: Purl.

Rows 25 to 44: As rows 2 to 21.

Row 45: Purl.

Row 46: Wk Pick-up row 1.

Rep these 46 rows once more.

On the final rep, wk Pick-up and cast-off row instead of Pick-up row 1.

Tier 16

Using CC, wk Pick-up row with increase (16 sts).

Row 1: Purl.

Row 2: Purl.

Row 3: Knit.

Rows 4 to 11: Rep rows 2 and 3 four times.

Row 12: Purl.

Row 13: Purl.

Row 14: Knit.

Rows 15 to 22: Rep rows 13 and 14 four times.

Row 23: Purl.

Row 24: Purl.

Row 25: Knit and mark this row.

Row 26: Purl.

Rows 27 to 48: As rows 2 to 23.

Row 49: Purl.

Row 50: Wk Pick-up and cast-off row.

Do not press/iron.

> **TIP**
> Why not add a tassel at each point for a sumptuous look? Turn to page 46 to find out how.

Simply pink

This wrap is pretty in pink, but would look lovely in a host of other jolly colours, too. A simple two-row pattern is repeated throughout, to great effect.

SIZE
- Approx 10 x 78in (25 x 200cm)

MATERIALS
- Sirdar Denim Ultra 60% Acrylic, 25% Cotton, 15% Wool (82yd/75m per 100g ball): 4 balls in 645 Madder Pink
- A pair of 10mm (UK000:US15) needles

TENSION
- 9 sts and 12 rows to 4in (10cm) over st st using 10mm needles.
- Use larger or smaller needles to obtain correct tension.

SPECIAL ABBREVIATION
- yo: yarn forward and around needle.

SCARF
Cast on 28 sts.
Row 1: (RS) K4, * p1, k1, yo, p2tog, k1, p1, k1, rep from * to last 3 sts, k3.
Row 2: K3, p1, * k2, yo, p2tog, k2, p1, rep from * to last 3 sts, k3.
Rep rows 1 and 2 until wk measures 78in (200cm) from beg, ending with row 2.
Cast off.

TIP
Try using a luxury evening-style yarn in silver or gold to create a scarf that will transform an outfit for a special occasion.

Windfall

Wear this gorgeous leaf-covered piece on a crisp and breezy day. Chase the leaves as the wind makes them flutter and swirl around, then hurry home to warm up by the fire.

SIZE
- Approx 6½ x 68in (17 x 173cm), including leaf fringe

MATERIALS
- Sirdar Click Aran with wool 70% Acrylic, 30% Wool (109yd/100m per 50g ball): 3 balls in 127 Spruce
- A pair of 5mm (UK6:US8) needles
- Two 5mm (UK6:US8) double-pointed needles

TENSION
Not critical. Yarn band tension: 18 sts and 24 rows to 4in (10cm) over st st using 5mm needles.

SCARF

Cast on 15 sts.

Row 1 (RS): K2, p2, m1, k1, m1, p2, k1, p2, m1, k1, m1, p2, k2 (19 sts).
(This row is the first row from cast on; when working through pattern, use row 1 given below).

Commence patt from written instructions

Row 2: K4, p3, k2, p1, k2, p3, k4.
Row 3: K2, p2, k1, yo, k1, yo, k1, p2, k1, p2, k1, yo, k1, yo, k1, p2, k2 (23 sts).
Row 4: K4, p5, k2, p1, k2, p5, k4.
Row 5: K2, p2, k2, yo, k1, yo, k2, p2, k1, p2, k2, yo, k1, yo, k2, p2, k2 (27 sts).
Row 6: K4, p7, k2, p1, k2, p7, k4.
Row 7: K2, p2, k3, yo, k1, yo, k3, p2, k1, p2, k3, yo, k1, yo, k3, p2, k2 (31 sts).
Row 8: K4, p9, k2, p1, k2, p9, k4.
Row 9: K2, p2, k9, p2, m1, k1, m1, p2, k9, p2, k2 (33 sts).
Row 10: K4, p9, k2, p3, k2, p9, k4.
Row 11: K2, p2, k3, k3tog, k3, p2, k1, yo, k1, yo, k1, p2, k3, k3tog, k3, p2, k2 (31 sts).

Row 12: K4, p7, k2, p5, k2, p7, k4.
Row 13: K2, p2, k2, k3tog, k2, p2, k2, yo, k1, yo, k2, p2, k2, k3tog, k2, p2, k2 (29 sts).
Row 14: K4, p5, k2, p7, k2, p5, k4.
Row 15: K2, p2, k1, k3tog, k1, p2, k3, yo, k1, yo, k3, p2, k1, k3tog, k1, p2, k2 (27 sts).
Row 16: K4, p3, k2, p9, k2, p3, k4.
Row 17: K2, p2, k3tog, p2, k9, p2, k3tog, p2, k2 (23 sts).
Row 18: K4, p1, k2, p9, k2, p1, k4.
Row 19: K2, p2, k1, p2, k3, k3tog, k3, p2, k1, p2, k2 (21 sts).
Row 20: K4, p1, k2, p7, k2, p1, k4.
Row 21: K2, p2, k1, p2, k2, k3tog, k2, p2, k1, p2, k2 (19 sts).
Row 22: K4, p1, k2, p5, k2, p1, k4.
Row 23: K2, p2, k1, p2, k1, k3tog, k1, p2, k1, p2, k2 (17 sts).
Row 24: K4, p1, k2, p3, k2, p1, k4.
Now wk row 1 as follows:
Row 1: K2, p2, m1, k1, m1, p2, k3tog, p2, m1, k1, m1, p2, k2 (19 sts).
The last 24 rows form the patt.

Commence patt from chart

Starting with row 2, cont working patt from chart until row 24 has been worked, then wk row 1 from chart.

The last 24 rows form the patt.

Both written instructions and chart

Rep 24 rows of patt until scarf measures approx 62in (158cm) from beg, ending with row 24.

Next row: K2, p2, k1, p2, k3tog, p2, k1, p2, k2 (15 sts).

Next row: K4, p1, k2, p1, k2, p1, k4.

Do not cast off – these 15 sts will be used for the leaf fringe.

LEAF FRINGE

With RS facing, using double-pointed needles, k first 3 sts from scarf.

**Make I-cord by slipping the sts to the other end of the needle, passing the yarn around the back of the work and k these 3 sts again (see page 47 for details). Rep from ** 4 times more, then wk in rows as follows:

Row 1: K1, yo, k1, yo, k1 (5 sts).
Row 2: P to end.
Row 3: K2, yo, k1, yo, k2 (7 sts).
Row 4: P to end.
Row 5: K3, yo, k1, yo, k3 (9 sts).
Row 6: P to end.
Row 7: K to end.
Row 8: P to end.

Row 9: K3, k3tog, k3 (7 sts).
Row 10: P to end.
Row 11: K2, k3tog, k2 (5 sts).
Row 12: P to end.
Row 13: K1, k3tog, k1 (3 sts).
Row 14: P to end.
Row 15: K3tog.

Fasten off.

Using double-pointed needles, k next 3 sts from scarf.

Complete 4 more leaves as before.

With RS facing and using double-pointed needles, pick up and k first 3 sts across cast-on edge of scarf. Complete first leaf as before and wk 4 more leaves to complete leaf fringe.

WINDFALL CHART

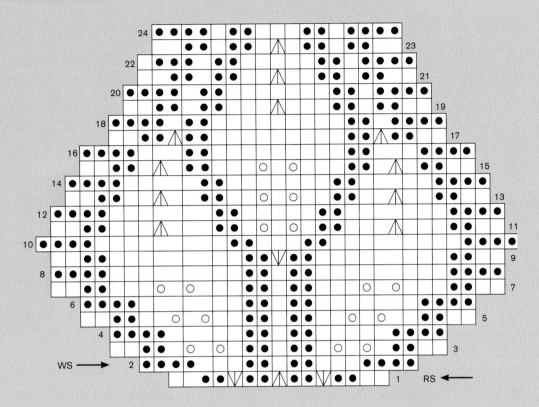

⊼ K3 TOG	☐ K ON RS, P ON WS
⊽ M1, K1, M1	● P ON RS, K ON WS
○ YO	

Tangaroa cowl

Winter wind and ocean spray are no threat to this textured cowl.
Inspired by New Zealand's black volcanic beaches, it can
be worn loosely around the neck and shoulders or up over the head.

SIZE
- Approx 14 x 74in (35 x 188cm)

MATERIALS
- Rowan Drift 100% Merino Wool (87yd/80m per 100g ball): 4 balls in 903
- A pair of 10mm (UK000:US15) needles

TENSION
- 9 sts and 12 rows to 4in (10cm) over st st using 10mm needles.
- Use larger or smaller needles to obtain correct tension.

COWL
Cast on 32 sts.

Commence stripe patt
Row 1 (RS): Knit to end.
Row 2: Knit to end.
Row 3: Knit to end.
Row 4: Purl to end.
Rows 5 to 8: Wk 4 rows in g-st.
Rows 9 to 12: Wk 4 rows in st st.
Rows 13 to 18: Wk 6 rows in g-st.
Rows 19 to 24: Wk 6 rows in st st.
Rows 25 to 32: Wk 8 rows in g-st.
Rows 33 to 40: Wk 8 rows in st st.
Rows 41 to 50: Wk 10 rows in g-st.
Rows 51 to 60: Wk 10 rows in st st.
Rows 61 to 68: Wk 8 rows in g-st.
Rows 69 to 76: Wk 8 rows in st st.
Rows 77 to 82: Wk 6 rows in g-st.
Rows 83 to 88: Wk 6 rows in st st.
Rows 89 to 92: Wk 4 rows in g-st.
Rows 93 to 96: Wk 4 rows in st st.
Rows 97 and 98: Wk 2 rows in g-st.
Rows 99 and 100: Wk 2 rows in st st.

Repeat rows 5 to 100 once more, then rows 5 to 60 again.
Knit 3 rows.
Cast off k-wise.

FINISHING
Sew cast-on and cast-off edges together.

TIP
Instead of joining the two ends together to make a cowl shape, you could leave it as a traditional long scarf.

Scarf and snood

You get two looks from one garment with this convertible scarf-into-snood. Wear conventionally or wrap twice and button. Imagine the fun you'll have choosing those buttons!

SIZE
- Approx 10¼ x 64in (26 x 162cm)

MATERIALS
- Debbie Bliss Cashmerino Chunky 55% Merino Wool, 33% Microfibre, 12% Cashmere (71yd/65m per 50g ball): 8 balls in 25 Ice Blue
- A pair of 6mm (UK4:US10) needles
- Cable needle
- 9 buttons

TENSION
- 20 sts and 22 rows to 4in (10cm) over cable patt using 6mm needles
- Use larger or smaller needles to obtain correct tension

SPECIAL ABBREVIATIONS
C4F (cable 4 front): Slip next 2 sts on to cable needle and leave at front of work, k2 then k2 from cable needle.

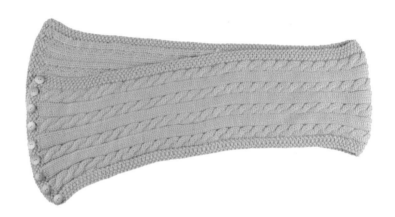

SCARF
Cast on 52 sts.

Commence moss st edging
Row 1 (RS): *K1, p1, rep from * to end.
Row 2: *P1, k1, rep from * to end.
Rep these rows twice more.

Commence cable patt
Row 1 (RS): K1, p1, k1, p1, (p2, k4) to last 6 sts, p2, k1, p1, k1, p1.
Row 2: P1, k1, p1, k1, (k2, p4) to last 6 sts, k2, p1, k1, p1, k1.
Row 3: As row 1.
Row 4: As row 2.
Row 5: K1, p1, k1, p1, (p2, C4F, p2, k4) to last 12 sts, p2, C4F, p2, k1, p1, k1, p1.
Row 6: As row 2.
These 6 rows form cable patt.
Continue until scarf measures approx 63in (159cm) ending with row 2.

Commence moss st edging plus buttonholes
Row 1: *K1, p1, rep from * to end.
Row 2: *P1, k1, rep from * to end.
Buttonhole row 1: K1, p1, cast off 1 st (there will be 3 sts on needle after cast off; the beg k1, p1, and the st left from the cast off), patt 3, (cast off 1 st, patt 4) to last 3 sts, cast off 1 st, patt 1.
Buttonhole row 2: Patt to end casting on 1 st to correspond with the cast-off sts of the previous row.
Next row: *K1, p1, rep from * to end.
Next row: *P1, k1, rep from * to end.
Cast off in patt.

FINISHING
Sew buttons on right side of beginning edge of scarf to correspond with buttonholes.

Button up

Keep your hands warm in the pockets of this ribbed scarf while watching your favourite sport. The collar features two yarnover buttonholes and the pockets are lined.

SIZE
- Approx 8 x 66in (20 x 168cm)

MATERIALS
- Sirdar Big Softie 51% Wool, 49% Acrylic (49yd/45m per 50g ball): 7 balls in 339 Cherry Pie (MC)
- Sirdar Snuggly Snowflake Chunky 100% Polyester (68yd/62m per 25g ball): 2 balls in 630 Milky (CC)
- A pair each of 10mm (UK000:US15) and 5.5mm (UK5:US9) needles
- Darning needle
- Sewing needle
- Thread for sewing buttons
- 2 buttons

TENSION
- 9 sts and 12 rows to 4in (10cm) over st st using 10mm needles and MC
- 14 sts and 19 rows to 4in (10cm) over st st using 5.5mm needles and CC
- Use larger or smaller needles to obtain correct tension

SPECIAL ABBREVIATIONS
- KFB: Knit into front and back of stitch
- PFB: Purl into front and back of stitch

SCARF
Using larger needles and MC cast on 26 sts.

Commence patt
Row 1 (RS): P2, *(k2, p2), rep from * to end.
Row 2: K2, *(p2, k2), rep from * to end.
These two rows form patt.
Cont in patt until wk measures 8in (20cm) from cast-on edge, ending with a WS row.
Next row: K to end.
Next row: P2, *(k2, p2), rep from * to end.
Cont in patt until wk measures 22in (56cm) from K row, ending with a WS row.

Wk collar
Row 1: K1, KFB, p2, yo, k2tog, patt to end (27 sts).
Row 2: Patt to last st, k1.
Row 3: P1, KFB, k1, patt to end (28 sts).
Row 4: Patt to end.
Row 5: P1, PFB, patt to end (29 sts).
Row 6: Patt to last st, p1.
Row 7: K1, PFB, p1, yo, k2tog, patt to end (30 sts).
Row 8: Patt to end.
Row 9: K1, KFB, patt to end (31 sts).
Row 10: Patt to last st, k1.
Row 11: P1, KFB, k1, patt to end (32 sts).
Row 12: Patt to end.
Row 13: P1, PFB, patt to end (33 sts).
Row 14: Patt to last st, p1.
Row 15: K1, PFB, P1, patt to end (34 sts).
Row 16: Patt to end.
Row 17: K1, KFB, patt to end (35 sts).
Row 18: Patt to last st, k1.

Row 19: P1, KFB, k1, patt to end (36 sts).

Row 20: Patt to end.

Cont in patt until wk measures 8in (20cm) from last inc row, ending with a WS row.

Row 1 (RS): P1, k2tog, patt to end (35 sts).

Row 2: Patt to last st, k1.

Row 3: K1, k2tog, patt to end (34 sts).

Row 4: Patt to end.

Row 5: K1, p2tog, patt to end (33 sts).

Row 6: Patt to last st, p1.

Row 7: P1, p2tog, patt to end (32 sts).

Row 8: Patt to end.

Row 9: P1, k2tog, patt to end (31 sts).

Row 10: Patt to last st, k1.

Row 11: K1, k2tog, patt to end (30 sts).

Row 12: Patt to end.

Row 13: K1, p2tog, patt to end (29 sts).

Row 14: Patt to last st, p1.

Row 15: P1, p2tog, patt to end (28 sts).

Row 16: Patt to end.

Row 17: P1, k2tog, patt to end (27 sts).

Row 18: Patt to last st, k1.

Row 19: K1, k2tog, patt to end (26 sts).

Beg with a WS row, continue in patt until wk measures 22in (56cm) from last dec row, ending with a WS row.

Next row: K to end.

Next row: K2, *(p2, k2), rep from * to end.

Cont in patt until work measures 8in (20cm) from K row, ending with a WS row. Cast off.

POCKET LININGS
(make 2)

Using smaller needles and CC, cast on 28 sts.

Work 13in (33cm) in g-st.

Cast off.

FINISHING

The K rows in the main part of the scarf create a folding ridge 8in (20cm) from the ends. Sew one pocket lining to the RS of the scarf, with the cast-on edges together, so that when this section is folded, the lining is on the inside. Fold the end of the scarf to the RS at the K row and sew in place to form a pocket. Work the other pocket in the same way. Sew on the buttons opposite the buttonholes in the collar section.

Techniques

GETTING STARTED

SIZE

The scarves and neck warmers in this book come in all sorts of different lengths and widths, but you can easily alter them to suit your personal taste. You can use more or fewer stitches, add or subtract length, or use a thicker or thinner yarn.

TENSION

Variations in tension can have a noticeable effect on the size of a finished scarf. However, as scarf size can vary to suit the individual, this is not really a problem. What's important is that you get a tension that makes a fabric that is neither too loose nor too dense.

MATERIALS AND EQUIPMENT

NEEDLES AND HOOKS

Most of the designs in this book are worked back and forth on standard knitting needles. Bamboo needles are useful if you are using a rough-textured yarn, as they are extremely smooth and will help to prevent snags. You may also need double-pointed or circular needles. Where crochet hooks are used, these are standard metal hooks that are widely available.

YARN

Scarves may be made in a huge variety of yarns. Wool or wool-mix yarns have the best insulating properties. If you are using acrylic yarn, you may prefer to choose one of the thicker designs.

Substituting yarn

It is relatively simple to substitute different yarns for any of the projects in this book. One way to do this is to work out how many wraps per inch (wpi) the yarn produces (see table).

It is important to check tension, so begin by working a tension swatch. Then wind the yarn closely, in a single layer, around a rule or similar object, and count how many 'wraps' it produces to an inch (2.5cm). For a successful result, choose a yarn that produces twice, or slightly more than twice, the number of wraps per inch as there are stitches per inch in the tension swatch.

TENSION REQUIRED	NUMBER OF WRAPS PER INCH PRODUCED BY YARN
8 sts per in (4-ply/fingering)	16–18 wpi
6.5 sts per in (DK/sport)	13–14 wpi
5.5 sts per in (chunky/worsted)	11–12 wpi

Knitting know-how

SIMPLE CAST-ON

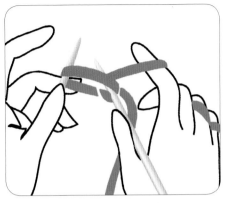

1 Form a slip knot by making a loop and pulling the free end of the yarn up through it to form a new loop. Put this on the left needle and pull the short end of the yarn to tighten. Insert the right needle into this loop and wrap yarn around it as shown.

2 Pull the yarn through the loop to create a new one

3 Slide the loop on to the left-hand needle. There are now 2 sts on the left needle. Continue in this way until you have the required number of sts.

CABLE CAST-ON

For a firmer edge, cast on the first 2 sts as above. When casting on the subsequent sts, insert the needle between the cast-on sts on the left needle, wrap the yarn around and pull through to create a loop. Slide the loop on to the left needle. Repeat to end.

THUMB METHOD CAST-ON

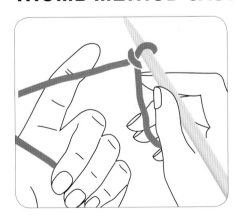

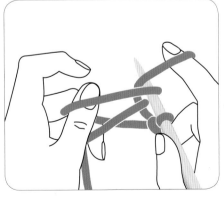

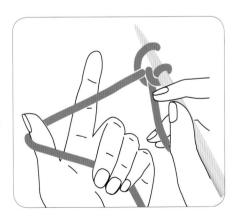

1 Make a slip knot some way from the end of the yarn and place on the needle. Pull the knot tight.

2 Hold needle in right hand and wrap the loose tail end around the left thumb, from front to back. Push the needle point through the thumb loop from front to back. Wind ball end of yarn around needle from left to right.

3 Pull the loop through thumb loop, then remove thumb. Gently pull the new loop tight using the tail yarn. Rep until the desired number of sts are on the needle.

KNIT STITCH

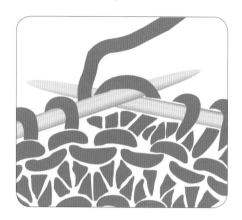

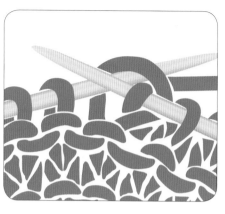

1 Hold the needle with the cast-on sts in your left-hand. Place the tip of the right needle into the back of the first st and wrap the yarn around as for casting on.

2 Use the right-hand needle to pull the yarn through to create a new loop.

3 Slip the newly made st on to the right-hand needle.

Continue in the same way for each st on the left-hand needle. To start a new row, turn the work to swap the needles and repeat steps.

PURL STITCH

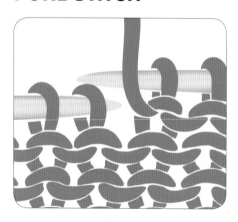

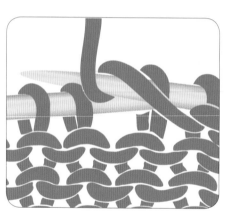

1 Hold the yarn at the front of the work as shown above.

2 Place the right needle into the front of the first st. Wrap the yarn around the needle in an anti-clockwise direction.

3 Bring the needle back through the st and pull through.

OTHER STITCHES

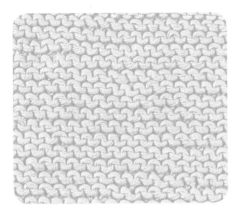

Garter stitch (g-st)

Knit every row.

Stocking stitch (st st)

Knit on RS rows and purl on WS rows.

Reverse stocking stitch (rev st st): Purl on RS rows and knit on WS rows.

Moss stitch (m-st)

With an even number of sts:
Row 1: (K1, p1) to end.
Row 2: (P1, k1) to end.
Rep rows 1 and 2 for pattern.

With an odd number of sts:
Row 1: *K1, p1, rep from * to last st, k1.
Rep to form pattern.

Single (1 x 1) rib

With an even number of sts:
Row 1: *K1, p1* rep to end.
Rep for each row.

With an odd number of sts:
Row 1: *K1, p1, rep from * to last st, k1.
Row 2: *P1, k1, rep from * to last st, p1.

Double (2 x 2) rib

With a multiple of 4 sts:
Row 1: *K2, p2, rep from * to end.
Rep for each row.

Colour knitting

INTARSIA

Blocks of colour are created by using the intarsia technique of twisting the yarns together at the back of the work with each colour change (see diagram). It is better to use bobbins than whole balls to prevent tangling. They are smaller and can hang at the back of the work out of the way. Once finished, ends are woven in at the back, and pressing under a damp cloth will help to neaten any distorted stitches.

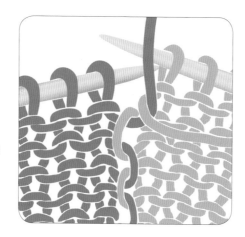

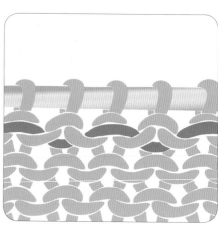

FAIR ISLE

Fair Isle knitting uses the stranding technique, which involves picking up and dropping yarns as they are needed. Unlike intarsia, they are carried across the row. Loops are formed along the back of the work, but these should not exceed about 5 sts in length. Make sure the loops are of an even tension or the fabric may pucker.

1 Begin by knitting with the first colour (A), which is dropped when you need to incorporate the second (B). To pick up A again, bring it under B and knit again.

2 To pick up B again, drop A and bring B over A, then knit again.

READING CHARTS

Most charts are shown in squares, with each square representing one stitch. Charts are usually marked in sections of ten stitches, which makes counting easier. When working in stocking stitch on straight needles, read the chart from right to left on knit (RS) rows, and from left to right on purl (WS) rows. Check carefully after every purl row to make sure that the pattern stitches are in the correct position.

PICK UP AND KNIT

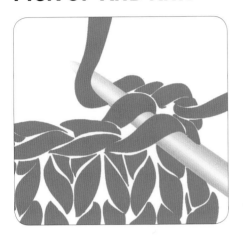

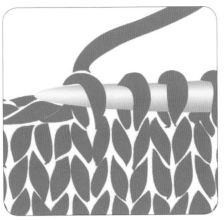

1 With RS facing, insert the needle under both strands of the edge stitch. Wrap the yarn around the needle.

2 Knit the picked-up stitch.

CASTING OFF

1 Knit 2 sts on to the right needle, then slip the first st over the second st and let it drop off the needle so that 1 st remains.

2 Knit another st so you have 2 sts on the right-hand needle again. Rep process until there is only 1 st on the left needle. Break yarn and thread through rem st to fasten off.

To cast off purlwise (p-wise), follow the same process, but with purl stitches.

Finishing touches

SEWING UP

MATTRESS STITCH

Place the pieces to be joined on a flat surface, laid together side by side with right sides towards you. Using matching yarn, thread a needle back and forth with small, straight stitches. The stitches form a ladder between the two pieces of fabric, creating a flat, secure seam.

STOCKING-STITCH JOINS

The edges of stocking stitch tend to curl, so it may be tricky to join. The best way to join it is to use mattress stitch to pick up the bars between the columns of stitches.

Working upwards or downwards according to preference, secure the yarn to one of the pieces you want to join. Place the edges of the work together and pick up a bar from one side, then pick up the corresponding bar from the opposite side. Repeat the process.

After a few stitches, pull gently on the yarn and the two sides will come together in a seam that is almost invisible. Take care to stay in the same column all the way. Do not pull the stitches tight at first, as you will not be able to see what you are doing.

GARTER-STITCH JOINS

It is easier to join garter stitch, as this has a firm edge and lies flat. Place the edges of the work together, right side up, and see where the stitches line up. Pick up the bottom loops of the stitches on one side of the work and the top loops of the stitches on the other side. After a few stitches, pull gently on the yarn. The stitches should lock together and lie completely flat. The inside of the join should look the same as it does on the outside.

BACKSTITCH

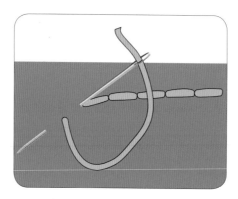

Work from right to left, bringing the needle up at point A, down at point B and then up at point C. Begin next stitch treating point C as the new point A. Repeat as required. Try to keep the distance between the stitches even.

TASSELS

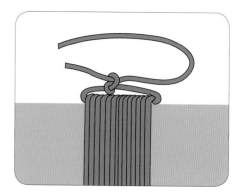

1 Cut a piece of stiff card so that the height is the required length of your tassel. Wrap the yarn around it several times, depending on how full you require the tassel to be. Secure this bundle with a separate length of yarn threaded through at one end, and tied to leave long ends. Cut through the bundle at the opposite edge.

2 Keeping the strands folded in half, remove the card. About a quarter of the way down from the fold, wind a separate length of yarn a few times around the whole bundle, including the long ends of the tie, to form the head of the tassel. Tie the two ends of this length of yarn together tightly. Trim all the ends of yarn at the base of the tassel to give a tidy finish.

FRINGING

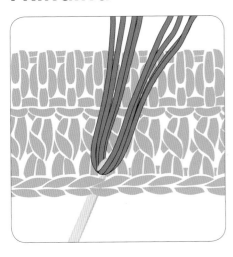

1 Cut a piece of stiff card so the height is the required length of the fringing. Wind the yarn around it – the number of times depends on how thick the fringe will be. Cut through the yarn at one edge of the card. Select the number of lengths of yarn you need for each tassel and fold them in half. Insert a crochet hook from the WS to the RS of the work where the fringe is to be and hook the folded yarn.

2 Draw the yarn some of the way through the work.

3 Now draw the cut ends through the loop to tighten. Trim ends.

I-CORD

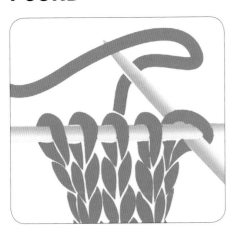

Using double-pointed needles, cast on the required number of sts – typically 5 sts. Do not turn work. Slide sts to the opposite end of the needle, then take the yarn firmly across the back of work. Knit sts again. Repeat to desired length. Cast off, or follow instructions in pattern.

Abbreviations

approx	approximately	**MC**	main colour	**st st**	stocking stitch	
beg	begin, beginning	**mm**	millimetre(s)	**tbl**	through back of loop	
CC	contrast colour	**P/p**	purl	**tog**	together	
cm	centimetre(s)	**p2tog**	purl two stitches together	**wk**	work	
cont	continue	**patt**	pattern	**WS**	wrong side	
dec	decrease(ing)	**psso**	pass slipped stitch over	**yd**	yard	
g-st	garter stitch, knit every row	**p-wise**	purlwise, as if to purl	**yo**	yarn over needle	
in	inch(es)	**rem**	remaining	*****	work instructions following *, then repeat as directed	
inc	increase(ing)	**rep**	repeat	**( )**	repeat instructions inside brackets as directed	
K/k	knit	**rev st st**	reverse stocking stitch: purl 1 row, knit 1 row			
k-wise	knitwise, as if to knit	**RS**	right side			
k2tog	knit two stitches together	**sl**	slip			
k3tog	knit three stitches together	**ssk**	slip 1 k-wise, slip 1 p-wise; knit these 2 stitches together through the back of the loops			
m	metre(s)	**st(s)**	stitch(es)			
M1	make 1: pick up loop before next st and k it through back of loop					

UK/US YARN WEIGHTS

UK	US
2–ply	Lace
3–ply	Fingering
4–ply	Sport
Double knitting	Light worsted
Aran	Fisherman/worsted
Chunky	Bulky
Super chunky	Extra bulky

KNITTING NEEDLE SIZES

UK	METRIC	US
14	2mm	0
13	2.25mm	1
12	2.5mm	–
–	2.75mm	2
11	3mm	–
10	3.25mm	3
9	3.5mm	4
9	3.75mm	5
8	4mm	6
7	4.5mm	7
6	5mm	8
5	5.5mm	9
4	6mm	10
3	6.5mm	10.5
2	7mm	10.5
1	7.5mm	11
0	8mm	11
00	9mm	13
000	10mm	15